WORLD'S SCARIEST CREATURES

BY JOHN LESLEY

FREAKY INSECTS

Gareth Stevens PUBLISHING

**Please visit our website,
www.garethstevens.com.
For a free color catalog of all
our high-quality books, call
toll free 1-800-542-2595 or
fax 1-877-542-2596.**

Cataloging-in-Publication Data
Names: Lesley, John.
Title: Freaky insects / John Lesley.
Description: Buffalo, NY : Gareth Stevens Publishing, 2026. | Series: World's scariest creatures | Includes glossary and index.
Identifiers: ISBN 9781482474114 (pbk.) | ISBN 9781482474121 (library bound) | ISBN 9781482474138 (ebook)
Subjects: LCSH: Insects--Juvenile literature.
Classification: LCC QL467.2 L475 2026 | DDC 595.7--dc23

Published in 2026 by
Gareth Stevens Publishing
2544 Clinton St.
Buffalo, NY 14224

First published 2025 by Redback Publishing

Author: John Lesley
Editor: Simone Saba
Designer: Redback Publishing
Original illustrations © Redback Publishing 2025
Originated by Redback Publishing

Acknowledgements
Abbreviations: l—left, r—right, b—bottom, t—top, c—centre, m—middle

We would like to thank the following for permission to reproduce photographs: Shutterstock; p8bl Kgbo, CC BY-SA 4.0 (https://creativecommons.org/licenses/by-sa/4.0>, via Wikimedia Commons); p14-15 m Bernard DUPONT from FRANCE, CC BY-SA 2.0 (https://creativecommons.org/licenses/by-sa/2.0), via Wikimedia Commons; p 17tl Donald Hobern, CC BY 2.0 (https://creativecommons.org/licenses/by/2.0), via Wikimedia Commons); p20-21c fStop Images GmbH/Alamy Stock Photo; p21bl Mark Marathon, CC BY-SA 3.0 (https://creativecommons.org/licenses/by-sa/3.0), via Wikimedia Commons, p24tl Wildan ardani, CC BY-SA 4.0 (https://creativecommons.org/licenses/by-sa/4.0), via Wikimedia Commons, 31br bogong moth, John Tann, flicker.com, https://www.flickr.com/photos/31031835@N08/10301606615

Printed in the United States of America

CPSIA compliance information: Batch #CSGS26
For further information contact Gareth Stevens at 1-800-542-2595.

CONTENTS

ZOMBIE ANTS

The *Cordyceps* fungus can turn ordinary ants into real-life zombies.

FACT

The zombie ant is powerless to resist once the fungus has taken over its brain.

The *Cordyceps* fungus is a predator that gets inside an ant and takes over its beahvior. The fungus controls what the ant does, forcing it to go to a place where there is a suitable temperature for the fungus to thrive. The fungus grows inside the ant until it can eventually make a hole and poke out of the ant's head or other part of the ant's body. The spores of the fungus can then be released, and they float off to infect other ants, turning them into zombies as well. After they are no longer useful as food and a means of transportation for the fungus, the zombie ant dies.

FACT

If the other ants see a zombie ant in the nest, they carry it away and dump it outside.

FACT

The *Cordyceps* fungus can also infect other types of insects, turning them all into zombies.

ASSASSIN FLY

FACT

Assassin flies have a long, thin abdomen and very large eyes.

Assassin flies, also known as robber flies, are aggressive hunters who eat other insects that they catch while flying. They grab prey with the claws on the ends of their legs, then inject it with a poison that starts to dissolve the internal organs. The assassin fly larvae are also carnivorous, looking for soft foods such as other larvae or insect eggs.

They range in length from about 0.12 to 2 inches (3 to 50 mm). They have a variety of habitats and are most numerous in regions with a warm and humid climate.

Assassin flies are also called robber flies.

FACT

Assassin flies can use their strong mouthparts to bite humans, but they do not see us as food.

TITAN BEETLE

Titanus giganteus

FACT

Adult titan beetles have a very short lifespan, often only a few weeks.

The titan beetle is one of the largest and most impressive beetles in the world. They have a robust and elongated body, with a dark brown to black exoskeleton that is hard and shiny. Their mandibles (jaws) are incredibly strong and can snap a pencil in half! Titan beetles have well-developed wings and are capable of flying.

Titan beetles are found in the tropical rainforests of South America, particularly in countries like Brazil, Colombia, Peru, Ecuador, and Bolivia. They inhabit lowland rainforests where they can find ample decaying wood, which is essential for their larvae.

When threatened, titan beetles can produce loud hissing sounds by forcing air out of their spiracles. They can also use their powerful mandibles as a defense mechanism.

FACT

The titan beetle is the largest beetle in the world.

FACT

Titan beetles have large compound eyes that take up around a third of the head.

SPINY LEAF INSECT

The spiny leaf insect looks just like a bunch of brown leaves. When it stretches itself out it is up to 7.8 inches (20 cm) long. Its legs, tail, and body segments are all shaped like brown leaves. In the wild, you can be right next to one of these big insects and not see it until it moves.

They are not harmful, and some people handle them and keep them as pets. Having such a big insect sitting on your hand can be very intimidating for some people, and it is difficult to overcome the urge to violently shake it off. Try not to do this if you are lucky enough to encounter a spiny leaf insect, as they are harmless and easily injured. Put your hand near a tree, and the insect will usually be glad to slowly climb away.

FACT

Spiny leaf insects do have little spikes on their legs, and these may cause a scratching feeling on your hand.

Spiny leaf insects are phasmids, like stick insects, but they look like leaves instead of twigs.

FACT

The female lays many small, dark gray eggs that drop to the forest floor, where they can last for a long time before they hatch.

CICADA-KILLER WASP

Exeirus lateritius

Unless provoked, cicada-killer wasps do not normally attack people.

FACT

These killer wasps look for the biggest cicadas to ensure the wasp grub is well-fed.

Wasps have a bad reputation for getting angry and stinging, but the habits and size of the cicada-killer wasp make it even more terrifying. These insects hunt and attack cicadas, which they sting and paralyze, but don't kill. After stinging it, the wasp struggles to drag its paralyzed prey along the ground and into its burrow. The female lays an egg on or near the fresh cicada, so that the young wasp has living food to eat when it hatches.

The wasp grows up to 2 inches (5 cm) long, and is the usual black, yellow, and brown color that many wasps are. Although they live in wild areas, they also hunt in suburban areas near people.

FACT

The entrance to the underground tunnel of a cicada-killer wasp can be 0.5 inch (1.2 cm) wide.

BULLDOG ANT

Myrmecia

Bulldog ants are easily angered, very aggressive, and their bite is excruciating. Once one of them bites, it sends out a signal by releasing a smell that tells all of the others to converge and start biting as well. Stand on a bulldog ant nest by mistake, and you will soon realize your mistake. One bite is painful but not deadly unless you are allergic to them. Multiple bites can be very dangerous.

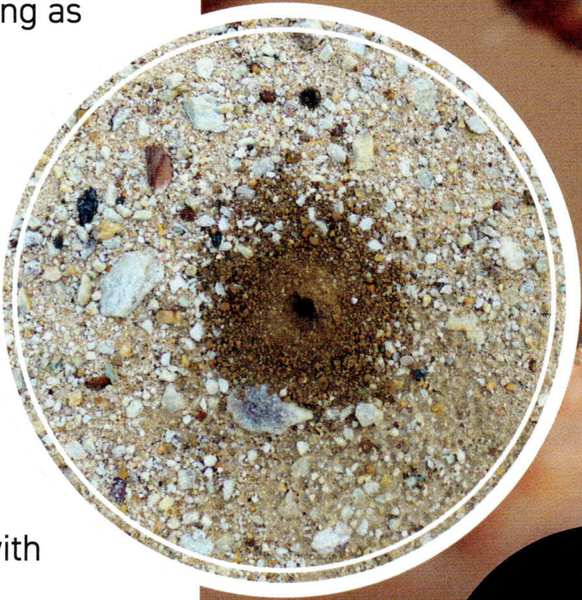

Bulldog ants grow to over 1.5 inches (4 cm) long. Their jaws are large and their bodies are black and orange. They build their nests very deep underground and with multiple chambers.

They pile up large mounds of dirt, up to 3.3 feet (1 m) across, on top of their nest. There are lookout ants posted at the opening, and they will let the others underground know if any living thing comes too close. Then they will all swarm out and attack.

If two queen ants encounter each other, they will fight to the death to rule the colony.

FACT

There is one queen ant in the nest. Her only role is to lay eggs, and all the other ants look after her.

FACT

When it attacks, the bulldog ant will hold on with its jaws, then twist its abdomen around to insert its stinger.

PROCESSIONARY CATERPILLARS

Ochrogaster lunifer

Covered in hairs that sting if you touch them, processionary caterpillars move around in large, stinging groups, searching for food.

They look as though they are covered in soft, gray hairs, but never touch one or you will regret it. The hairs are very hard to remove from your skin and will stick into you, continuing to sting and causing a lot of pain.

Processionary caterpillars are the caterpillar stage of bag moths. They will travel in search of food, all moving together in lines that can be many feet long. They can also be found all curled together in a massive stinging bunch.

FACT

The caterpillars turn into moths that are also covered in stinging hairs.

Just being near these caterpillars is dangerous since their hairs can blow off in the wind.

FACT

Take care if investigating a strange, big lump on a tree. It might be a group of resting hairy caterpillars.

HERCULES MOTH

Coscinocera hercules

The Hercules moth is enormous, with a wingspan up to 12 inches (30 cm) wide. They are brown, black, and white, which camouflages them on branches when they are not moving. Their body is covered in hair that looks like fur.

Hercules moths are not harmful to humans, so just enjoy the sight of one flying off if you get the chance.

FACT

The larvae are pale blue with bright yellow spikes, and grow to over 4 inches (10 cm) long.

FACT

The adult moths have no mouthparts and so cannot eat. They live for less than two weeks.

FACT

The wings of the adults have transparent patches on them, like little windows.

WITCHETTY GRUB

Endoxyla leucomochla

FACT

Also called a cossid wood moth grub.

Witchetty grubs are a well-known bush food in Australia, where Indigenous people have been roasting and eating them for thousands of years. Today, adventurous restaurants will include witchetty grubs on their menu. The term witchetty grub is sometimes used to describe other sorts of big, white grubs of moths and beetles.

The moth eggs hatch into witchetty grubs, or larvae, that like to feed on the roots of an acacia tree called a witchetty bush. When they are ready to pupate, the grubs stop eating and create a protective cocoon as they undergo a change into a moth. The adult moth has the coloring of tree bark.

FACT

This moth can grow to have a wingspan of over 6 inches (15 cm).

FACT

Witchetty grubs live in burrows under trees, where they eat the roots.

The adult moth breaks out of its pupa and must wait a few minutes for its wings to fill with fluid before it can fly. The moth's only purpose after reaching this part of the life cycle is to find a mate and breed. Then they die.

At this adult stage of life, the moths have no mouth or biting parts, so they are not harmful to humans. These huge moths used to be common, even in the suburbs, but the advancing development of towns and the resultant removal of trees has contributed to a decrease in their numbers.

RHINOCEROS BEETLE

Xylotrupes ulysses

FACT

Although the male beetle's horn makes it look intimidating, these beetles are not at all harmful to humans.

Rhinoceros beetles are found worldwide, particularly in tropical and subtropical regions. They are prevalent in Asia, Africa, the Americas, and Australia. Glossy black or brown, strong and formidable, the male has horns on its large head and thorax, and it uses them to fight with other males. The smaller females do not grow horns, making them look like big Christmas beetles, to which they are related.

Rhinoceros beetles can grow up to 2.8 inches (7 cm) long. The larvae, or grubs, are just as big. They eat rotting plant material and are sometimes found in suburban compost bins, although the forest floor is their natural habitat. After pupating under the ground, the beetle emerges. It is an omnivore, eating plants as well as dead animals.

Rhinoceros beetles hiss when they are fighting, or if you pick one up.

FACT

The sturdy exoskeleton enables the males to knock each other over when fighting.

GIANT COCKROACH

Macropanesthia rhinoceros

The Australian giant burrowing cockroach will sit happily in the palm of your hand, rather than scuttling off like the faster cockroaches that live in our kitchens. It has a segmented body that is glossy brown, and it can grow up to 4 inches (10 cm) long. Just the thought of touching such a large cockroach would horrify some people.

The giant cockroach lives in leaf litter in forests and does not want to take up residence in people's homes. It does not bite or spread germs. It has an important role in its habitat, eating decaying plant matter to recycle it. They have a flat, oval shape, which makes it easy for them to move through dead plant material and leaves on the ground.

The female gives birth to little cockroaches, rather than laying eggs like most insects do. The young are called nymphs, and they stay in the female's underground burrow until they are old enough to look after themselves. The burrow can extend for more than 3 feet (0.9 m) down into the ground.

FACT

Giant cockroaches are native to Australia, adding to the long list of big and scary wildlife that live there.

Also called the rhinoceros cockroach.

FACT

Giant cockroaches can suffer from obesity if they do not move around enough.

HOW ARE INSECTS SPECIAL?

Insects are in the animal group Arthropoda, which includes crabs, lobsters, centipedes, and spiders.

WHAT IS DIFFERENT ABOUT INSECTS?

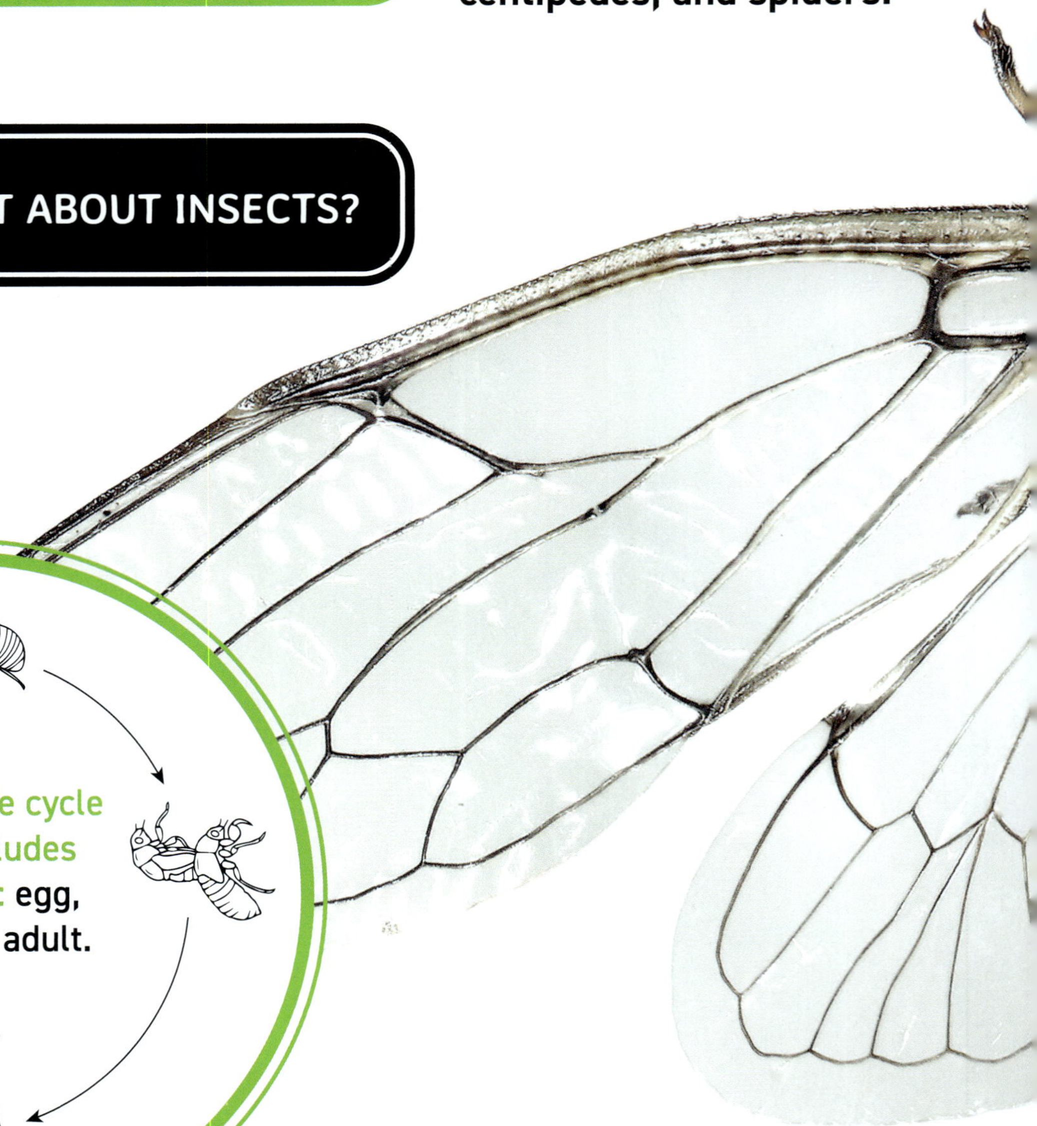

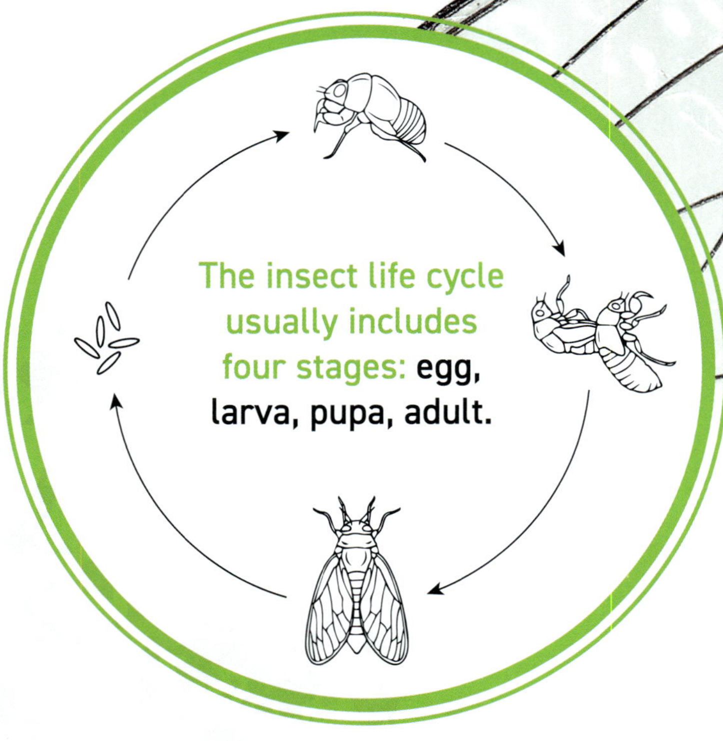

The insect life cycle usually includes four stages: egg, larva, pupa, adult.

There are two sensory antennae on the head.

Insects are the only invertebrates that have wings and can fly.

Instead of internal bones, insects have a hard shell called an exoskeleton that gives them their shape. Insects need to shed this hard skin as they grow bigger.

The adult form has six legs.

The three body parts are: head, thorax, abdomen.

CREEPY-CRAWLY PETS

Fear of creepy-crawlies is very common and stops many people from ever considering keeping insects as pets.

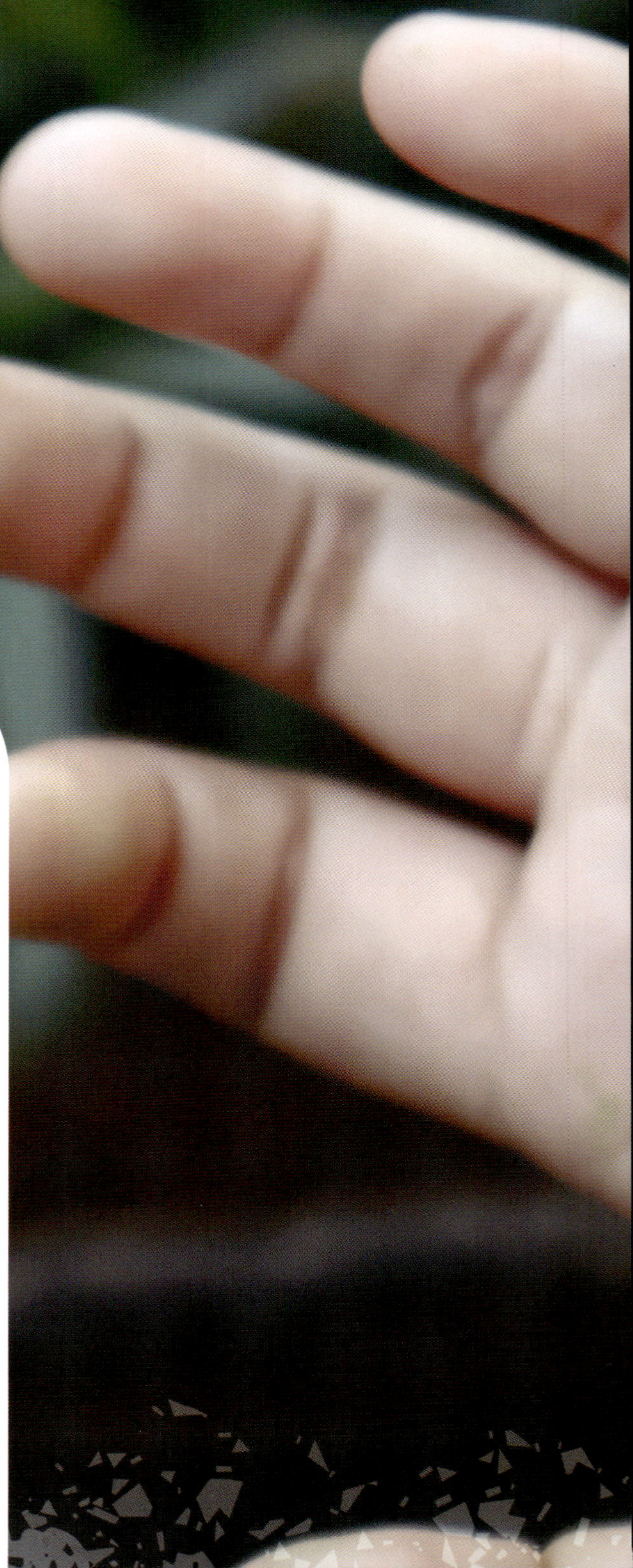

If you want a pet that likes cuddles and welcomes you when you get home, then an insect is not for you. If you are fascinated by these small but impressive creatures, then keeping a pet insect can be one of the most interesting things you can do.

Insects are good at escaping from cages and disappearing somewhere into the house. They need special diets and conditions to survive, so you will need to do some research before even thinking about keeping a creepy-crawly.

As with all native creatures, never take an insect from the wild. You should seek a specialized insect pet seller instead.

SPINY LEAF INSECT

MORE INSECTS

SHIELD BUG
LADYBUG
DRAGONFLY
PRAYING MANTIS
BOGONG MOTH
CHRISTMAS BEETLE

GLOSSARY

Insect Word List

excruciating very painful

exoskeleton external body support

formidable frightening and powerful

intimidating frightening

nymph juvenile insect

obesity condition of being overweight

paralyze cause to be unable to move

pupate go into a condition in which all the insect's body parts change

spiracles opening in the exoskeleton

INDEX